LUTALICA

Poems Warming the Soul Like Winter Sun

MANNAT SINGHANIA

BookLeaf
Publishing

India | USA | UK

Made with ❤ on the BookLeaf Publishing Platform

www.bookleafpub.in

www.bookleafpub.com

Dedication

To my,
Future Self,
My Family,
And My Buddies,
Always.

Preface

Hey, you!
Yes, you.

The fact that you're reading this means you've somehow stumbled into my chaotic little world of poetry—welcome!

This isn't your typical, sit-straight-and-read-seriously kind of book. Nope. Think of it more like scrolling through a bunch of deep, late-night thoughts, random bursts of emotions, and maybe even a few existential crises (in a somehow poetic manner). Some poems might hit like a sad song on repeat, others might feel like an inside joke between you and the universe. Either way, I promise it won't be boring. Read it however you want—front to back, back to front, or just randomly flipping to a page and letting fate decide your mood for the day. No rules here, only vibes.

<u>*Warning*</u>*: You might be obsessed with it!!*

So, grab a cup of coffee (or your favorite snack, a healthier option works too) and get comfy.

<P.S> *laugh, reflect, cry a little (or not), and most importantly—just feel.*

With overwhelming passion,
Mannat.

Acknowledgements

Shoutout to my parents—my OG sponsors and life coaches. Thanks for funding my snacks, tolerating my questionable sleep schedule, and believing in me even when I doubted myself. This book exists because of your endless love (and occasional emotional blackmail).

<u>Cc:</u> To my utmost nemesis, my elder sister Kashti di, the creative genius behind my book cover and occasional idea bank—you really understood the assignment.

*Thanks for making my words look
as good as they sound.*

I. Poetry: Through my glasses

A book of words, woven in verse,
A patient struggling for a caring nurse-
Days and days, this book of words,
The poem for a poet is like a sherd.

Some readers find, joy in reading,
Some readers find, joy in meaning,
But all of them come to one-
The poem for a reader is like a war won.

These complex words, not a simple play-
A collection of poems, an eternal survey-
Try and try till you know,
A simple trick to this "complex show".

At dawn, the lines may cloud the mind,
By dusk, you may enjoy, a windfall find,
A poet writes, but who is free?
The poem, in turn, rewrites me.

II. A Language Gone

Words and sounds, and letters along,
Make me up- decades long.
People use me, as a balloon,
Utter and 'talk', then toss my cocoon.

Pages of history love my charm,
But those pages rest, in a dust-wrapped farm.
Some beings last used me, decades long,
A being last used me, in a song.

Culture, History all bygone,
I too shall walk, by morning's yawn.
Words and sounds, and letters along,
Walk with me, wherever you belong.

III. The Silenced Dictionary

In the world of truth, a 'word-play' seen-
A game of chess, but without a queen.
'Freedom' and 'Revolt', reduced to sin-
"A trivial issue"-What is this scene?

Pages are thin, with hollow echoes,
A crafted calm, by a blood-red rose.
Poets wake, but after the call,
Verses erased, a month of fall.

Silence stood, but speeches rose-
A game of chess, but empty rows.
All we knew, was 'Yes' and 'No'-
A world of truth, now long ago.

IV. A Playlist

A crowd of songs, but all silent-
I am a playlist, stranded in an island.
Melodies made, re-valuation done,
Songs are made,
And outrun.

Hopes brim, yet dim,
(No one there, "Maybe someone in a gym")
I am a playlist, waiting to be played-
A song unsung, a note delayed.

V. Three days in traffic

Day one, stuck in traffic slow,
Buildings, factories and industries show.
All around, a city sky-
Full of skyscrapers, tall and high.

As the green light shows, I'm off,
But the city around me, still aloft.
In awe, I ponder what I've seen
the marvels of this modern scene.

Day two, Traffic's much the same,
But boredom now begins to claim,
The hours tick by without a sound-
The city's beauty now unbound.

As the green light shows, I'm off,
But dust and grass everywhere, people cough.
Now I understand, what I've seen,
I'm now bored of this modern scene.

Day three, Traffic is still moving
People are shouting, fighting and abusing,
But as i sit, I start to see,
The people who make up this city.

The red light shows, "Merciless, Inexorable"
The police man shouts, "I'm not answerable"
The poor man moves around, knocking the window,
"I'm not giving you anything" says the Lindo.
The street vendors, the homeless too,
Those struggling, striving to push through-

In these three days of traffic strife
I've learned the values that define life,
Progress, beauty but also care
For those around us, everywhere.

So, as I drive through this place
I'll keep these lessons in my grace
Tomorrow, I will again return to this traffic
And hope to learn many more classics.

VI. The Cycle of Classics

Pondering over the cycles of life though,
Pictures of some elements show,
But, deep within me I know,
Life must go on, so-

A tea, no sweet,
Not my classic!
But for those, "their life without magic"-
Yet these people are the ones who choose joy,
The journey of life in a healthy toy.

A pot of earth,
Not my classic!
But for those, "lost in traffic"-
Yet these pots withstand rain,
The journey of life, and without complain.

A library of books,
Not my classic!
But for those, "They belong to the Jurassic"-

Yet these books are your best friends.
The journey of life never ends...

VII. All of Us

All of us, are born as a family,
Then we live happily,- 'What a fantasy'!
And, then there's this little child,
Lost in a loop, without a map,
His mouth wrapped with some of those app.

All of us, are born to make friends.
Creating hashtags-'New trends'!
And then there are two friends sitting,
Echoing sounds, but those of clicking.

All of us, are born as humans-
Unknown to the living allusions,
Now, we have all made our own, little huts,
At the end of the day, there are only 'Some of us'.

VIII. The Dichotomy of Fatherhood

Some days bring joy, some days bring strife,
They say- 'He is always right',
I wonder, why they say it so,
He is not always perfect though.

He goes to work and comes home late,
Then mom screams- "My fate"!
He forgets his promises many a times,
Leaving us to deal with all his 'crimes'.

He never answers the call, neither calls back,
As if he is earning daily, bundles of lakh.
Now i ask you-"Is he always right?"
I know, you don't have an answer, that's alright.

Some days bring joy, some days bring glee,
They say- "He is always wrong you see"
I wonder why they judge him so-
He is not always, flawed though.

He works hard to provide for us all,
His love and care, he does recall,
He may forget a promise or two,
But he always makes it up anew.

He may be busy with work and life,
But, he's always there in times of strife,
Now, I answer you- "He is not always wrong"
I hope this reply makes your belief strong.

So, here's to the fathers the heroes of our life,
For all they do, for all they strive,
A love that's unwavering, a bond that's strong,
For this we honor them in this song.

IX. A letter from the Calendar

Dear owner,
My ribs are gone,
The pages are torn,
It's time to go-
A new square has come, so-

I mention the days-
I helped you know,
Your joy, your sorrow and about the snow-
The clock, just feels like "sometime ago".
Look for my last words given below.

The last thing to show you is a fresh, new path
The newly made ribs, with a fresh, new math.
"Thanking you,
Yours sincerely"-are,
the last words i say,
Ending the letter, on a December day.

X. I don't live near the.....

I once lived near the mountains
Now, I live near the woods,
The dreams, woven once-
Are now enclosed in the hoods!

I once imagined a life in the mountains
But now I miss their echoing tales,
I only get the sound of a despairing heart-
which now feels stuck under a veil.

Now,
I get the musky scent of the earthly beings,
In this lush green forest, where hopes brim,
But, soon I see the sight of the autumn woods
which resembled those of the mountain hoods.

I realized being impaired all these days.
Now, the dreamy fallacy unhoods-
I once left those mountains-
Now, I am leaving these woods.

XI. Will they return?

I have heard many stories,
Songs of the past as well as present glories,
Parents, two children and me too,
A family long ago, the family I knew,
In this wood-thatched structure lies my life,
A family of five, through my eyes-
They laugh, they shout, as the walls hear,
My life without them, a life too queer-
A humming whisper still heard, in the walls,
No warmth remains, in the snowy stalls,
Cotton in the ears, a creaking sound,
I still long for that warmth around-
Time drifts on, yet I remain,
Will we ever meet again?

XII. Diary of the Sand

Dear Diary,
The bell has rung!
Blue hour has come!
There is nobody around-
It feels no fun!

The sun shines bright,
on the sandy shore,
The clinging sounds:
Bring fright and more.

The waves once splashed,
Shells of laughter and play,
Now I find peace-
At the end of the day!

The bell has rung!
Blue hour has come!
There is nobody around-
It feels so fun!

Thanking,
Each of you,
"The End"- I say,
The end, of a 'Glorious Day'.

XIII. From Ink to Ashes

Footsteps with a muffled roar,
The glory of me like never before,
Lines and dots on paper though,
Years and Years, yet people show.

Footsteps crack, whispers rack,
No one now, a silent track-
Concrete marvels in reality though,
Years and Years, yet no one show.

XIV. Five Questions

In the sacred space, where wisdom flows,
A disciple queries, seeking truths untold,
Five questions poised, profound and deep,
Life's mysteries unravel in the guru's keep.

(Disciple)
Life's like a fragile blossom,
Which stands on a shaking column,
So, why does it unfold in such a way,
and then finally to wither away?

(Guru)
Life's like a lotus on the river's flow,
It withers, yet seeds of eternity sow,
In each petal, a sacred design,
which makes the flower truly divine.

(Disciple)
In the tapestry of time,
why is there this weird design-

Where the threads of joy and sorrow intertwine,
Painting a canvas, both bitter and fine?

(Guru)
In time's tapestry, threads align,
Joy and sorrow, a dance divine,
Each moment woven in destiny's loom,
A dance of fate, with a cosmic tune.

(Disciple)
Amidst,
the sound of guns and roar of wars,
Why do we see-
Corpses lying far and far?

(Guru)
Soldiers brave, the tempest roar,
Political wrangling, a turbulent lore-
Yet, in the dance upon death's brink,
They find courage in duty's link.

(Disciple)
Death is inevitable, this we know,
Someday, we all need to go-
But what happens after death,
I would like to know about death's flow.

(Guru)

After death's curtain, the soul takes flight,
Beyond one can imagine, in eternal light.
Like a bird, who just learned to fly,
It soars higher and higher transcending the sky.

(Disciple)

Now, it's time,
To ask about the most hostile foe-
About something,
We all want to know!

(Guru)

It's the jealously and ego,
which resides deep within,
Casting shadows-
On the soul's serene skin.

The disciple, in awe, absorbs the lore,
In the guru's wisdom, seeks and explores,
Life's questions answered, a journey starts,
In the loom of knowledge, a disciple's heart.

XV. White feathers

Cooing pigeons all around,
In awe of grains found,
To carry letters in battle ground-
Filled with secret mound.

Mother's leg tied with a small paper,
She flies and flies amidst milky vapor,
Children amazed, look upon the sun,
But the latter was amidst the roar of gun.

Lead balls ricocheted in the ground,
Touched the mother with a tiny sound-
White feathers could be seen falling all round'
A healthy soul, now impound.

Children wait, yet sun moves
"A silent wind", felt the youths,
Children amazed, look upon the sun,
But the latter melted, amidst the roar of gun.

XVI. Ghats

I-witness,
The water's splashing sound,
The black petals of marigold,
A dance of saffron all around-
In this land of mystic old.

I-witness,
A library of light, the sound of gold
Cooing all round' me,
The color of tea, "a mud of mold".

Yet again-
I-witness,
Another light, which lights all night long.
The echoes of cries, from pyres along,
The cooing continues
Deep within those-

In the Ghats of Banaras,
Beauty Beholds!

XVII. The Legend of a Comet

YEARS AND YEARS,
Hence, time has passed-
A comet fell, with a bomb-like blast.
Words fell out of the comets mouth
Like water flows, in parts of south.

Wonders of heaven, Wonders of hell,
He showed some shapes, which looked like shells.
The shells had memories, and images trapped,
Like, people nowadays in mobile tabs.

Shell one, had images of cosmic wonders,
Man-made marvels and humanly blunders.
Yet, what we saw was a hue of colors-
The journey of time, through last few summers.

Shell two, showed visuals at eternal speed,
Some splendid shows, quite agreed!
Up spoke the comet with a fierce roar,

"Don't touch the shell"-to a boy just four!

Shell three, came up, in just no time,
With texts and speeches-a poetic rime.
It had tears in it, of people dead,
It's color had no magic, a simple red.

YEARS AND YEARS,
Hence, time has passed-
A comet fell, with a bomb-like blast.
The comet has since, not been seen,
Like some old creature in the marine.

XVIII. Concrete Pasture

Drops dripping,
Roots beating,
Branches rustling,
Wind tickling,
And, a healthy soul,
In **concrete crippling.**

Hay found on the pavement green,
A bunch of cows sitting in between,
Hay gone,
Roots seen,
A healthy soul,
In **concrete crippling.**

XIX. Heirs of Light

Both of us are **heirs of light**,
Yet I am near, and you, at some height-
Why just can't I be like you?
A life adrift, a life anew.

I am stuck in a colorless land,
With little life around me, "You won't understand"-
Clock beats, day goes-
My life is made of silent echoes.

I cling to some-body,
They say, I am a mere copy
Yet all I wish is to float away,
To dreamlike lands, a forever stay.

Both of us are **heirs of light**,
Yet I am far away, and you, at the site-
Why just can't I be like you?
A life on land, a life anew.

.

XX. "Perfection!"

Sculptors and artists, there are many though,
The art half-done, is the best art I know,
Half-bloomed flowers and uncarved stones,
The art of nature, a beauty unknown.
The incomplete rainbow and the spiderwebs,
The art of nature- Incomplete shapes.
Crack in the old walls, and rough edges too,
The art of nature- A sacred view.
A count of marks on breathing beings,
Bring old-new memories, gloomy feelings.
Yet,
The canvas of nature, has many brushes left,
A masterpiece waiting, for a 'manly theft'!

XXI. Seasons of a day

Dust playing in a beautiful light,
Cherry blossoms bloom- a palate white:
The morning like a spring though,
The call of cuckoo, time to go.

An orange glow in the bright luster,
Burns the mantle, the shiny buster.
Lenses and windows hide in a cover,
The clock runs slow, a time to suffer!

Yellow seen in green fields,
A crisp mist, for a time to heal,
Long distances for a new place,
Dreams ring the stories, of some old race.

Darkness orders to be alone,
Think of you, without a phone,
For cuckoo still checks the clock,
Waiting for the morning knock!